Enough

Stories of God's Creation & Love

Danelle Wasden

Illustrated by: Anna Fernández

The primary song mentioned in one of the short stories was from (Children's Songbook, 34-35)

The scriptures were quoted from the Old Testament Authorized King James Version.

These stories are written from the memory of the author and may vary from the memory of those involved. Some names have been changed in the stories to protect the identity of the individuals.

ISBN: 978-1-7355267-1-3

First Printing: August 2020

Dedicated to family and friends that helped me along the way. Most importantly a huge shout out to my husband that always encourages me to reach for my dreams!

-- Danelle Wasden

Table of Contents

Light &
Darkness
Hope

And God saw the light, that it was good: and God divided the light from the darkness. And God called the light Day, and the darkness He called Night.

Genesis 1: 4-5

The sun was high, and the day was hot as my dad, brother, and cousins loaded the not-so-trained horses up with all our camping gear. Butterflies darted around in my stomach as the sleeping bags flew off the mustang's back for the seventh time. I tried distracting myself by drawing pictures in the dry dirt. My dad would cuss and yell as they gathered the sleeping bags and tried to put them back on the mustang.

By the time all the horses were loaded with our camping gear, I'd pretty much decided that I didn't want to go on this sheep trail (our family camping trip through the mountains where we trailed our sheep without any access to vehicles). My nerves were shot because of the rodeo that was happening all around me.

My dad hollered, "Mount up!"

I hated to disappoint him.

There was something inside me that feared what he thought. I couldn't exactly explain it, but it had always been there. I got on my horse, which was the gentlest horse we owned, and my sister sat behind me. We fought about who was going to drive, but I was older, so I got to be first. I pulled our gentle giant as far away from the pack horses as possible because I did not want to be anywhere near them when the camping gear went flying.

As soon as everyone mounted, we headed out. My dad led, of course. We rode up the dirt trail, and everything seemed to be going smoothly. The sun was lowering in the sky a bit, so it wasn't as hot as when we were loading the mustangs. My nerves had settled somewhat. I was enjoying the ride and singing with my sister.

We had just headed into a small grove of trees when a branch caught one of the pack horses in the side. This caused quite a stir. It ran and jumped and bucked and bucked. And bucked, until the pack was completely off. My heart was racing again. I was sure my horse was going to buck me and my sister off even though our horse had not bucked a day in its life.

"Hold still, sis," I whispered. "Don't say a word."

We sat frozen on our horse, tense as little field mice trapped by a cat. I watched my horse's ears to make sure they were not pinned back like it was my life on the line. I'd seen enough horses pin their ears back and then buck that I knew what I was looking for. When he would move his ears at all, I would gently rub his neck and whisper, "Good boy, good boy."

Thirty minutes later, my dad had the pack horse ready to go again. We started back on the trail and were moving along again. The sun was even lower in the sky, and the temperature was perfect. I relaxed a bit more. I was actually even enjoying myself. We continued through the mountains as if the day was never going to end. We enjoyed the sunflowers. We chatted about the joys of summer. We even made up a few songs.

My brother led a pack horse. His horse was tired of the horse behind him and gave it a swift kick. This sent his pack horse bucking. The tents fell off. The food went flying. Nothing was left on the horse's back. We paused again. By this time, the sun was just heading behind the mountain.

My dad seemed more rushed this time as he repacked the horse. He kept an eye on the sun that soon became a sliver. We had just a pinch of light left as we headed out again.

"Are we almost there?" Rachel asked.

"I think we're close." I didn't know the trail well. I was supposed to be brave and smart because I was older, but I didn't feel brave or smart.

The darkness grew. The mountains of Star Valley, Wyoming did not radiate light like the streets of the big city. We would soon be in complete and utter blackness. We continued to ride. I could no longer see much, except the butt of the horse in front of me. Rachel was crying behind me. I could feel the tears welling up in my eyes.

The darkness seemed to come right into my heart. The only hope I had of us making it to our camping spot was the faith that I had in my father. He never let me down. He was smart. He'd ridden these mountains since he was a young boy.

We rode in silence for what seemed like hours. I held on to the horn of the saddle. Rachel's arms were tightly wrapped around my waist. I was glad she was with me. She kept me warm. Without the sun beating down on us, it was teeth-chattering cold. My body grew tired. I thought maybe we should just stop and camp where we were, but I remained silent.

In the silence, I heard the sound of a stream. We were getting close. Once we crossed the stream, it was just a football field's distance away from where we camped.

I was towards the end of the pack string and heard screaming from up ahead. It wasn't like scared screaming but total anger screaming. My mom had just got bucked off into the water. I'm pretty sure my dad was in for it.

She was fuming. It was all his fault because we left later than we should have. He didn't load the pack horses right. He probably didn't even breathe right at that moment. Rather than getting back on her horse, she walked the rest of the way. Even though there was tension in the air that was as thick as the darkness surrounding me, I felt hope and excitement because I knew we were practically there.

Climbing off the back of my horse, I felt a sense of relief. We were done riding in the dark. The solid ground under my feet spread peace throughout my whole body. I felt like the stars shined brighter now that we were off our horses. We unsaddled and unloaded the packs.

I was in charge of starting a fire. This was one of my favorite jobs. Searching in the dark, I found the fire ring. I searched for wood along the hill side. Finding just enough, I started the fire.

In just a few minutes, we had light. Not only did we have light, but we had warmth. I felt relief and hope. Our journey through the dark had ended. Our source of light and warmth was secure.

After the fire was blazing and my body was hot, I rolled out my sleeping bag. I rarely set up a tent because I loved to sleep under the stars. This moment was no exception. I finally crawled into my bag.

As I said my prayers that night, I was grateful for a safe journey. I was grateful for the hope that the sun would rise again in the morning. I was grateful for the safety of my family. I was grateful for the darkness that would make it easy for us to sleep.

I realized that night, that God separated darkness and light for our benefit. Because we are *ENOUGH* and worthy of God's love, he allows us to live in a world with light and darkness that bring peace, love, and hope.

Water
Power

And God said, Let the waters under the heaven be gathered together unto one place, and let the dry land appear: and it was so.

Genisis 1:9

The hot sun beat down on us as we backed the pontoon boat down the boat ramp. I had not been to Lake Powell since I went with my parents on a houseboat fifteen years earlier. The houseboat was sold, but the wonderful memories of Lake Powell stuck with me, so my siblings and I decided that we wanted to experience it again with our kids.

We had the boat loaded with tents, food, sand toys, and lots of children; nine children under the age of eight, to be exact. The boat was big enough for ten adults. We figured since our children were small, seven adults and nine children was just about right. Usually, Lake Powell brought me so much excitement, but this time I was a little more nervous. Before, I was the kid. I didn't worry about anyone else. I rode tubes, wake boards, played in the sand, and sun tanned.

This time, however, I packed food, loaded life jackets, rubbed on sunscreen, and changed diapers, all the while, telling everyone how much fun we were having. We zipped up life jackets and headed out to find the perfect camping spot. We all enjoyed the journey across the water.

Finally, we found a place that was perfect. It had sand. It was in a little cove. We pulled up with our overloaded boat and set up camp. It was fantastic. The water was warm. The kids were playing, and we were having a grand time. We decided that we would go see some ancient ruins that were just a small boat ride away, about ten miles from where we were camped.

Overloaded, we slowly made our way up the lake. As we continued on our journey, the water became more and more rough. It was bouncing us quite a bit. We finally got to the cove where the ruins were. It was a little calmer but still very wavy for our overloaded pontoon boat.

Everyone but Joe, my brother-in-law, was holding onto a kid because he was the driver. He kept saying, "We are doing great. We are going to be fine." I believed him. In the cove, we tied our boat up to the bathroom dock that was anchored in the middle. The boat banged against it as the wind continued to whip through the cove. We watched boats going by out in the main channel. We couldn't decide what to do. Should we continue on to the ruins that were deeper into the cove or head back before the wind picked up more and the waves grew larger?

Honestly, I did not know what to do. We had so many little lives counting on us. We continued getting beat against the dock by the waves and the wind. My sisters' babies were crying. An unspoken panic surrounded our boat.

We couldn't just keep sitting there. We decided to head back.
Little did we know that the waves in our little cove were mild.
Joe drove the boat into the waves, so they wouldn't tip us over
sideways. He navigated us quite well.

We nervously made it to about half a mile from our campsite.
The wind continued to whip us. I watched as each swell would
take our little boat up and back down. I prayed in my heart. I
prayed in my head. I prayed that the Lord would keep us safe. The
only person that would speak was Joe. He kept saying, "We will
be ok." At this point, I wasn't sure. Our little boat seemed like a

small animal about to be devoured by its predator. The waves got bigger and bigger. I thought to myself, "Our life jackets will keep us all afloat. We will be fine when the boat gets swallowed."

We were just about to head around the rock wall when a houseboat was coming past us. It was big. The waves didn't seem to bother it. It was not going to get swallowed. It gave me a little bit of hope, like a security blanket. The people on the boat had their cameras out, filming us. We must have looked ridiculous. Sixteen people on a baby boat, barely making it above the swells of the waves.

I thought, "If we go under, they will come save us." Just as this thought crossed my mind, I watched the nose of our boat go under. Water came flooding back. Joe yelled, "Everyone move to the back!"

I was already in the back. I grabbed onto my oldest son while holding my toddler. I knew we were going under. My heart was racing. Water covered my feet. Seconds passed as everyone flew to the back of the boat. The nose popped back up. Joe said, "We are going to be fine."

The water flooded over the sides of the boat and back into the wavy lake. We were still above water. Yes, we were still above water!

My niece, Lana, was yelling, "My shoe! My Shoe!" Two pink shoes were floating away in the waves behind us. One was hers, and one was mine. I did not care. Everyone was still on the boat, and we were still floating. Everyone stayed towards the back of the boat so that the nose would stay up. We finally made it around the rock wall, and the waves seemed to calm down.

Soon, we were back at our camp. The wind was still blowing. One of our tents had been blown over. I was scared still. The power of the water was real. We were lucky to be alive. We were lucky to be together. I did not want to get back onto that boat. Land was my security.

Water has power. We need water to drink, to bathe in, to travel on. Water can ruin homes, damage crops, and kill. Water falls from the heavens. It comes up from the ground. Water has power. It has more power than I ever thought possible.

"I am smart," I thought. "I am in control," I thought. What I really know is that God is in control. He saved us that day on our overloaded pontoon boat. He controlled the power of that water. He allowed our overfilled pontoon boat to make it back safely to camp through the waves and wind. He loved us *ENOUGH* to protect us.

Plants Growth

And the earth brought forth, grass, and herb yielding seed after his kind and the tree yielding fruit, whose seed was in itself, after his kind: God saw that it was good.

Genesis 1:12

As a fourteen-year-old girl, I decided that I wanted to plant a garden for one of my church projects. I loved when my mom planted peas. We hadn't had a garden for a couple of years, so I decided that this was something I could do. My parents humored me in this endeavor. They allowed me to create a place in our yard for a garden spot. We brought in railroad ties. We brought in dirt. I planted all the seeds that I thought would grow in Randolph, the coldest place in Utah. I would be lucky if the garden didn't freeze in the middle of June.

I had no question in my mind that my garden would grow. I watered it. I did a little weeding. That was not the fun part, so I did not do it well. It did begin to grow. I grew quite a few radishes that first year. I also grew some peas. One thing that I was not short on was weeds. They grew and grew, but among those weeds were some of the vegetables that I had planted. I got the peas that I loved. For several years, I replanted this garden because it did so well the first year. It did not do as well every year, but we always got a little something out of it.

After I got married, I was so excited to have my own garden and my own yard. I once again brought in railroad ties. I used these railroad ties for my flower garden. I had two tiers along the south side of my house. I planted flowers. I planted bushes. I planted a few peas. I spent many hours tending my plants so that they would grow. I loved my little flower beds in the front of my house.

My very favorite flowers were sunflowers. I planted them when I first moved in, and they grew back every year. They got thicker and thicker. I did not have to do much work for these. They grew on their own. They got watered with the rest of the flowers and then reseeded themselves. I have come to realize that some plants need lots of tending to grow, and some need very little, but they all need water and sun.

We, like the seeds, all have the ability to grow. Some of us need lots of extra care, while others seem to spring up with just a little water and sun. There are times in our lives when we seem to thrive on our own and other times when we need someone there to hold us up and keep us growing. God loves us enough to send others to tend us and water us and help us grow.

He knows that we will have struggles and that weeds will get in our way, but He also knows that we will become stronger as we withstand the weeds, the wind, the frost, and the drought. He is watching over us. He is there when we are ready for help, and He allows us to bloom into the beautiful people He created. He created each of us to be *ENOUGH*.

Sun

Moon

Stars

Trust

And God made two great lights; the greater light to rule the day, and the lesser light to rule the night: He made the stars also.

Genesis 1:16

My dear friend questioned God and His existence but was answered with the majesty of the moon and the stars. There are times in life when trials come our way that cause us to question the very existence of God. At this time of life for my friend, she was questioning everything. Her life was falling apart. Everything she believed from when she was a young girl seemed to be crumbling before her eyes. She felt completely suffocated and didn't know what to believe anymore. She was never so scared in her entire life. She felt like she was going to explode.

During this uncertain time in her life, she remembers going for a walk in the middle of the night because sleep escaped her. The stars she remembered as a child were very bright, but where she currently lived, they never got quite that bright, but on this particular night, the stars shown bright like her childhood memories. The moon seemed to shine with a special glow as well.

As she walked through the tall pine trees and noticed the stars and the moon, she prayed. She didn't know who she was praying to. She hoped that there was someone there listening to her. She remembers thinking, "What is true? What is not true?" She was panicked and pleading for an answer. She didn't even know if who she was shouting to was really there.

At that moment she stopped, silent. With tear filled eyes she looked up at the stars. They were brighter than she had seen in a very long time. She had the overwhelming feeling that there was no way that the stars and the moon were created by accident. A flood of peace washed over her. Her heart was light again. It was the stars, the crisp air, and the silver sliver of the moon that brought her peace and an answer that she had been searching for, for a very long time.

I headed to my sixteen-week doctor appointment with my 16 year old sister, Maggie, and my 2 year old son, Dexter. We were carefree and waiting in the doctor's office. The only thing I was nervous about at this doctor appointment was weighing in.

I hated seeing the scale crawl upward with every appointment. I completely avoided weighing myself at home. They called me back, and Maggie stayed with Dexter in the waiting room. I went back and weighed in. Wow! I had done fabulous this time. I wasn't gaining nearly as much weight as I did with my first son.

I then went back to my room and waited for the doctor. He took out his little heartbeat finder and came over to me and started searching. It seemed to take him longer than normal this day. I didn't think anything. After a little bit, he said that we should do an ultrasound but not to worry that sometimes this tool just couldn't pick up the sound.

Seconds into the ultrasound he knew that the baby had passed away. I started crying. Maybe he was wrong. He should check again. My doctor said many comforting things, but nothing seemed to register. My husband and I had tried for so long to get this baby.

This shouldn't be happening.

Because the baby had been gone for a couple of weeks, the doctor set me up to deliver the baby at the hospital. He suggested that I go get something to eat and that he would call me when they were ready for me to deliver. Completely numb, I went out to the waiting room to face my sister and my son.

I called my husband and my parents, and they rushed over the mountain to Logan. While we waited, we went to Café Rio. I hardly ever go there anymore, because it reminds me of that day.

The doctor soon called me back, and my parents and husband arrived. My parents took Maggie and Dexter home, and we headed up to the delivery floor. I couldn't believe this was truly happening.

Was I not a good mother? Why would God allow this to happen to me? If he didn't want me to have a baby, I shouldn't have gotten pregnant.

The nurses and doctors were kind. They proceeded like it was a normal delivery. My husband, Dustin, was there by my side and never left. I kept trying to wrap my head around why this had to happen. People came in and asked what we wanted done with the body and gave us plenty of options. They asked if we wanted to hold the baby when it was delivered.

I just wanted it all to go away. I wanted to run away, but I was lying in a hospital bed delivering a baby that shouldn't come for at least another twenty weeks.

The baby soon came. They prepared him and brought him in for us to hold. I tried to hold him, but I lost control of all emotions. They could see that it was not good for me, so they took the baby.

It was early in the morning when we left the hospital and drove home. My heart was filled with sorrow, which quickly turned to anger. For the next several months, I was mad at God. He had no right to do that to me. He had no right to allow this to happen. I remember going to worship and telling him that he owed me. He allowed this to happen to me, and it wasn't fair. I often sat crying on my kitchen floor in despair. Other women were having babies around me. Their babies were healthy and strong.

I decided to train for a race. This was a good outlet. It helped with my anger.

After my race and after I had given up fighting God for what had happened to me, I had the opportunity to go worship in His temple. I opened my heart to Him. I quit asking why this happened to me. Instead I asked what to do next in my life.

God answered me. He brought to my mind the words of a very familiar primary song. "Have faith, have hope, live like his Son, help others on their way." These words ran through my head over and over. I knew what I needed to do. I pleaded with God to forgive me. I decided to move on that day. I decided that life was better when I had faith, and when I had hope. I knew I needed to try and live like Christ, and most importantly, I needed to help others.

Just as the sun, the moon, and the stars come up every day and every night in their greatest majesty, God will show up in our lives with great majesty, if we open our hearts and minds to see Him, to feel Him, and to hear Him. He loves us *ENOUGH* to give us experiences that we need.

Animals Love

And God made the beast of the earth after his kind, and cattle after their kind, and everything that creepeth upon the earth after his kind: and God saw that it was good.

Genesis 1:25

Leaning against the wooden fence feeding my new little bum lamb with a bottle, I could hardly hold the excitement in my little ten-year-old body. During lambing, I always fell in love with the

cute little black and white lambs. Because our herd had mostly white lambs, a black and white lamb rarely had a bad mom and ended up being bummed. This year, I got lucky. This was the cutest little lamb in the whole entire world, and he was mine. I could hardly believe my luck. Not only was he mine, but he loved me.

He didn't care that I had funny crossed teeth. He didn't care that I wore hiking boots every single day. He didn't care that my family owned a business that everyone in town hated, and when you live in a small town of less than 1,000 people, that pretty much makes you an outcast.

He also didn't care if I was the fastest girl in my class. He didn't care that I always got good grades. He didn't care that I listened to my parents. He just loved me for exactly who I was.

It took me several days to teach my lamb how to suck the bottle. He was used to his mother, and this was a bit different. Every morning and evening, I would take my bottle out and feed him. Eventually, he became a great little bottle sucker. He would run over baaing, so excited to see me. He would follow me around. He would guzzle the milk down and beg for more.

One morning, I went out to feed my little lamb, and he did not come. It was so unusual. I looked around and didn't see him anywhere near the fence or in the tall grass. I decided to look over by the canal. As I walked up the canal bank, there he was, not moving.

I ran closer and saw that he was wet and stuck.

He looked bloated like many lambs I'd seen before. He was dead. He had gotten stuck in mud getting water and ended up drowning trying to get out.

My little heart broke. I couldn't stand it. This couldn't be happening. I decided to run. I ran out of the field and up the road. I didn't make it far. Breathless and blind from crying, I just laid down on the gravel. I buried my face in my hands, curled up in a ball and cried. My most favorite lamb ever had died because I didn't take care of it the way that I was supposed to. He loved me, and I failed him.

My mother eventually saw me lying in the middle of the road and came out. She asked what was wrong. I told her. She hugged me. She loved me as well, pretty unconditionally, too.

Because of her experience with ranching, she knew that animals die. She had empathy for me, but she reminded me that this was what happened when you lived on a ranch. She said that it was good to love, even if our hearts get hurt. Rather than never feeling the good to avoid the bad, we should enjoy the good and endure the bad.

I have never forgotten that lamb. He had a pure love for me. Dogs, cats, lambs, calves, and any pets have an unconditional love for their caretakers. They are loyal and unjudgmental.

To feel unconditional love as animals feel it, judgment must be removed. We, as humans, are capable of this because Christ did it. He is our perfect example. He does not care who we are or what we have done. He loves us just as we are. As we learn to see ourselves with less judgement, we will also see others with less judgement and feel the love that is possible.

We are *ENOUGH* and so is everyone else.

Child of God

And God said, Let us make man in our image, after our likeness: and let them have dominion over the fish of the sea, and over the fowl of the air, and over all the earth,

Genesis 1:26

Failure. We all go through it. It seems that the older we get, the more that it becomes unacceptable. When we are just learning to walk as toddlers, we can fall 100 times and still get back up. We do not question if we are worthy or if we are loved because we fall. Even when we learn to talk and our words do not come out quite right, we don't quit. We don't question our worthiness. Then we begin school. We are expected to learn to read, write, etc. We begin to see that other kids can do it better.

My son was the smartest, fastest, best human on the planet at the age of three. I knew he was.

"He is going to be the valedictorian of his class. He is going to be the star on the basketball team. He is going to be the kindest kid in the whole world. He is basically going to be better than

anyone else in the whole world at everything." These were my thoughts as a first-time mother.

Then he started school. He hated kindergarten. He practically bawled every day before school and begged not to go. I made him go anyway. His teacher said that he was doing fine.

The next year, he changed schools. After the first week of school, his teacher called me in and asked if they had done anything at his last school because he was so far behind. She was worried because he didn't pay attention well enough.

My heart was crushed. My child was not the smartest in his class. He wasn't even the second smartest. He was at the bottom of his class, and he didn't know how to pay attention like the other kids! Didn't she know that he was the best kid in the whole world at everything?

After crying tears of frustration, anger, and disappointment, I realized something. All of my false ideas that my son had to be the best compared to the rest of the world were not good. They were not good for him, and they were not good for me. I realized this the moment I was driving home from school. My son was perfect just the way he was. He did not have to be the best in the whole world at everything. The only thing he had to be good at was being him. He was enough just because he was my son.

That first grade year, we worked hard to help my son have success, not because I wanted him to be the top of his class, but because I wanted him to be the best him he could be. He made huge leaps and bounds. He grew tremendously. Even if he had not grown, I would still have loved him. I loved him because he was mine. This is how God's love works. He loves us because we are His. He created us.

We are *ENOUGH* because we are God's children.

Sitting on the hard benches in my high school gymnasium, I anticipated the principal announcing this year's high school royalty. Surely, I would be one of them. I mean, my class only had twenty girls. It wasn't like I was in one of those big schools that had 500 girls to choose from. I sat there acting like it really didn't matter, but it did. My mom was homecoming queen. She was cool.

All the boys loved the homecoming queen. It meant you were beautiful. It meant you were the most popular girl in school. It meant you had no problems. It meant you were what every girl in school wanted to be. It meant you were better than all the rest.

First, they announced the second attendant. It wasn't me. It was one of my best friends, Jessica. My heart sank just a little. Next, they announced the first attendant. It wasn't me. It was another one of my best friends, Sherrie. At this point, I knew it

was a long shot for me to be the queen because the most beautiful, most popular, and actually one of the nicest girls in the school had not been chosen yet. She was going to get it unless someone cheated on the ballot. The principal announced her name. It was who I knew it would be. I cheered for my friends as they went up there with their beautiful smiles, gorgeous hair, and perfect lives. I pretended that I was so thrilled for them.

I wasn't. I was completely jealous. I decided that homecoming royalty was stupid. It was just a silly tradition. I also knew that I was a bit odd. I marched to the beat of my own drum. I generally did what I wanted and didn't care what anyone thought. Watching the royalty celebrate, I knew that I wasn't popular. Don't get me wrong, I wasn't hated or stuffed in the corner and made fun of, but I wasn't one that everyone looked at and thought, "I want her life. She is so cool!"

As life progressed, I married a man that didn't care that I

wasn't homecoming queen. He loves me anyways. I've had five children. They don't care that I wasn't homecoming queen either.

More important than that, I learned that everyone was created by God. God created the world and his greatest creation was me. It was you. It was all humans. We are His Children. We are all equal. He did not create anyone better than anyone else even though some of us are homecoming queens and some of us beat to our own drum.

Comparison to others causes a lack of self-worth, but when we drop the comparison and see each other's differences as God sees them, we will see that God has poured out blessings that are fit for a queen to every single one of us.

You are different, and you are *ENOUGH*.

Rest

Gratitude

And God saw everything that He had made, and, behold, it was very good.

Genesis 1:31

I had just finished my senior year of track. That season seemed especially miserable. Most practices were inside because there was so much snow on the ground, and it was too cold outside. Most meets I had snow blowing in my face as I tried running to the finish line.

I was tired of being the senior class president and listening to complaints about the senior trip or the endless discussions about what we should wear to graduation and who was going to do what. I was done with all of it. As soon as I graduated, I was moving away and never coming back.

A few months later, I was in Salt Lake City living in an apartment with three girls I didn't know and playing volleyball for a small community college. I was free from Randolph. I was a big city girl now. I could do what I wanted, when I wanted. I was on my own.

Honestly, I was scared. I had very little experience driving in the city. Luckily, my apartment was very close to campus, and Albertson's was less than a block away. I could drive to school and the grocery store without getting lost and hopefully without running into the billions of cars in the city. What in the world were all of these people doing?

I didn't admit to anyone that I was scared. I was determined that this life had to be better than home, even though I was doubting it with every car that I passed, along with the long hair left in the drain by my roommate that I had to clean out so that the water wouldn't pool up as I showered.

Starvation was also a big concern. Living off Froot Loops wasn't as fun as I thought it might be. I was missing the home cooked meals that my mother always had ready when I got home from practice. My aunt that lived about forty-five minutes from Salt Lake City would invite me over for dinner on Sunday afternoons, and I always took her up on it. I ate more than enough and put on my freshman fifteen very quickly (Froot Loops and late-night Denny's trips were the main problem), so obviously I was not starving.

I made it through the first few months of college. I spent many hours crying in my car, more homesick than I could ever imagine. At home, I was a big fish in a little pond. Everyone knew me, and I had people that loved me there. Here in the big city, I was a little fish in a big pond and lost in the crowd. I quickly realized how grateful I was for that cold place called home. It wasn't as bad as I had made it out to be.

We don't usually realize how blessed we are until something is taken away from us or our circumstances change, whether it is our living conditions, our health, or the relationships that we have. When we are grateful in all of our circumstances, we will find rest and peace. Even as a lonely college student, I eventually found gratitude in that delicious bowl of Froot Loops, fun roommates, and exciting adventures.

When we have gratitude in our lives, we have *ENOUGH*, and we are *ENOUGH*.

Enough

Remember the worth of souls is great
in the sight of God;

Doctrine and Covenants 18:10

God's creations are everlasting evidence of the incredible worth that each and every individual has. He created majestic mountains. He created powerful oceans. He created beautiful trees. He created birds that sing.

But His greatest creation was YOU!

He created you in His own image. No matter what you do or have done, your worth is set because you are God's child.

You are loved, and you are *ENOUGH*.

About the Author

Danelle Wasden has a passion for helping people dream. She lives with her fun, loving husband and five children in the small town of Randolph, Utah. She is a member of The Church of Jesus Christ of Latter-Day Saints. She loves to be physically active, play in the outdoors, and work hard. She believes that life is as good as you make it!

CPSIA information can be obtained
at www.ICGtesting.com
Printed in the USA
LVHW071200111220
672555LV00071B/512